The Sto

# The Story

*A Single Mother's Journey
and Life Lessons*

Roxie Gaultier

**To order additional copies of this book, contact:**
Xlibris
1-888-795-4274
www.Xlibris.com
Orders@Xlibris.com
778288

# CONTENTS

Dedication ................................................................ vii

Preface ..................................................................... ix

The Beginning of the Beginning .............................. 1

Lessons ..................................................................... 7

The Quiet House ..................................................... 13

Happy Hour at The Spot ........................................ 15

The Reconciliation ................................................. 17

The Final Break Up ................................................ 25

Moving Out Again and Again ................................ 29

The Betrayal ........................................................... 35

Forgiving ................................................................ 45

The Call .................................................................. 49

My Calling .............................................................. 53

Stuck in the Middle ............................................... 61

My Survival ............................................................ 71

My Sun Moon, and Stars ....................................... 75

The Back Story ....................................................... 79

Love After Heartbreak .......................................... 91

Epilogue ................................................................. 95

# DEDICATION

To my friends & family, thank you for your continued love
and support and for always being there.

To my kids, thank you for choosing me to be
your mommy and for giving me purpose.

# PREFACE

*"He is a wise man who does not grieve for the things which he has not, but rejoices for those which he has."*
— *Epictetus*

WHAT AN AMAZING life I have. It's not by any means extravagant or glamorous, yet it remains amazing. I haven't traveled the world, yet I have seen so much. I don't have a graduate degree, yet I've learned so much. My biggest teacher has been my experiences in this crazy classroom we call life. It hasn't always been kind or easy but I wouldn't be who I am today if it always were. I wouldn't be surrounded by the people around me today. So, would I trade those experiences and lessons for a more extravagant or glamorous life? Not for all the tea in China.

This is my story. My path. It is one that can only be told by me because I walked it. Yes, it involves others but they have their own story to tell. Others are part of my story because I did not come down this road alone. That is the beauty of it all. We can be a part of something while remaining who we are. This story is told from my point of view. It is me sharing some of the events of my life with you. It was more of a challenge to write than I initially anticipated. It required the revisiting of some not so pleasant times in my life, but in the end it reminded me of how far I've come. This does not make me special. It makes me real. It teaches me that there's always a lesson to be learned if we pay close enough attention. Some things in here I've never shared with anyone, and some only a small circle of trusted friends are aware of. However, there's something to be said about purging. It is incredible, the plethora of emotions I experienced putting this together. It was healing to say the least. My best therapist has been the journals I've kept since my last pregnancy in 2006. I am sharing the good, the bad and the ugly here, because it is time. Come, let me take you on my journey.

# THE BEGINNING OF THE BEGINNING

*"Every new beginning comes from some other beginning's end."*
— *Seneca*

LIFE IS A funny thing. You can be striding along, humming to the tune in your head thinking everything is perfectly fine and BOOM, you're knocked off your feet and the next thing you know you're on the floor looking up like WTF!!! I'd like to start with one of the biggest WTF moments in my life. The moment that catapulted my life in a whole other direction.

Picture this if you will. It is July 2006. I am a 31 year old mother of four. I have been married for eleven and a half years to the man I thought I'd be married to for the rest of my life. Our youngest child and newest addition to the family is 3 week old Sebastian. I am striding along, humming to the tune in my head thinking everything is perfectly fine and BOOM, my husband comes home from work and says we need to talk. Yup! You guessed it. That talk left me on the floor looking up like WTF!!! The 'Talk' if you haven't figured it out was the, "I want a divorce, I don't want to be married anymore" talk.

We lived in a waterfront two story 4 bedroom, 2 ½ bath house we built two years earlier in Fort Myers, Florida. We are in a gated community which in hindsight gave me a false sense of security. It was a beautiful home which still wasn't fully furnished. It was a Wednesday evening, I had been home all day with the kids. The big kids were already in bed. I was upstairs in the baby's room getting him settled for bed. I remember Robert coming home asking me to come downstairs. I remember him sitting me on the couch in the family room where just 3 weeks prior, I laid on the floor giving birth to our youngest son. Sitting on that couch across from him, I felt numb. I knew whatever was coming wasn't going to be good. It was in the air. That doomsday feeling. Still in his work suit, I sat across from him as he started. Once I realized where the conversation was going, I went cold, felt like someone just kicked the life out of my body. I didn't want it to be true. It couldn't be true. "I'm filing for divorce Roxie" are the words I heard as I slowly started to return to my body. "I just can't do it anymore" he continued. His reasons for wanting the divorce he said was a combination of my lack of drive to go back to school and to lose the weight I'd put on since our first son Quincy was born. He was free of blame of course because he had been the perfect husband. He didn't actually say that last part but that is how it registered. How could he be saying this? I thought. He said this marriage was forever. I'm not just talking about our vows, I'm talking about the promises. The talks we had after we'd argue about something, or when we heard about someone we knew getting divorced. "No one gets a divorce in my family" he would say. "We can fight and argue but we figure that shit out." So why is he talking about divorce now? We just had a baby". It was one of those moments where you start looking around waiting for Ashton Kutcher to jump out saying you're getting punked, but you know that's not going to happen. So you start waiting to wake up because this isn't real, until you realize you are wide awake. The only thing this can be is a waking nightmare. That is one thing you don't know how to escape. You don't know how to get out of it or make it stop. So you start bargaining. You bargain like a condemned man, bargaining for his life with his executioner. Except your pleas fall on deaf ears. I was on my knees crying, pleading and begging. Not something I can ever remember doing in the past, but there I was, pleading for the life of my marriage. "I'll go back to school" I said. "I've been thinking about doing it anyway. I'll lose weight. I'll try harder" I begged. Doing and saying anything I could to save us. I got nothing back. His mind was made up. It had been made up way before he uttered those words, way before he walked through the door that night, and I eventually realized, way before our new son was born. I just wasn't privy to it.

Everything else that happened that night is a blur. We spent the rest of the night in bed talking. We talked about how we would proceed, about what it would be like dating other people. We used to host a yearly new year's eve party.

It's something we had been doing for nearly a decade. That's one of the things we talked about. "What about the party?" I asked. "People will have to make other plans" he said. "It'll be fine". That sucks I remember thinking. Here I was worrying about people having to rearrange their NYE plan right in the middle of my life was falling apart. It was all so surreal. "Why don't we still do something just you and I on the 31st". He said. "Are you crazy?" I replied. "That's like six months from now. You'll probably have some new chick by then". I continued. "Well that won't matter", he interrupts. "Regardless of what's going on or who we're seeing, we'll let that person know we have plans". "Yea right" I chimed. "What are we going to say, uh sorry new person, I have a date with my ex husband/wife tomorrow, I can't ring in the new year with you?" "Exactly" he says, "if they don't understand that's on them". "Epa-w fou" I thought in Creole dismissing him, which loosely translates to "I see you've lost your damn mind". We changed the subject, but talked some more. We made love. Yes, we made sobbing love the night this man came home telling me he was leaving me because I was no longer good enough. We woke our eldest daughter Priya to break the news to her. We cried, she cried, we consoled her and put her back to bed.

About the kiddies. Priya, our oldest is the ultimate girl's girl. She's ten years old and is the happiest little girl. She's cute, sassy and she knows it. Indya, almost seven, is a terror, though equal parts sweet and adorable. She has the biggest heart. She follows her sister around like a shadow. Indya is that little girl who can be playing dress up with her sister one minute, and the next you'll find her rolling in the mud with her little brother. She's the only child of mine to throw tantrums. Needless to say, she's a handful. Quincy, almost 5 is for lack of a better word, the perfect child. His sisters hate that about him. If asked, they would say he is a tattletale. He follows the rules to the T and for a boy that was a welcomed blessing. Quincy is the child who at 645pm will remind his sisters that it's almost time for bed. What kid does that? They would lose it when he did things like that. This boy lives by the clock. Our baby Sebastian is only three weeks old. He is the newest addition to our little family. He was born in less than ten minutes on the family room floor before the paramedics could even get there. No this was not on purpose. All natural and no epidural. Not my idea of a good time. I thought I was going to die. He's a happy baby, but a savage at the breast so breastfeeding didn't last long with him.

As the days and weeks passed, Robert moved out, and immediately filed for divorce. In fact, he served me exactly one week after 'the talk'. Shit just got real didn't it? I immediately registered at the local community college to start my prerequisites for nursing school. The kids didn't understand any of it really. Priya, though we talked to her, I don't think had full understanding of it all. Indya and Quincy being as young as they were didn't understand the concept of divorce, and Sebastian was of course just a baby. Sadly living separately was going to be his norm. Once it was clear that my marriage was truly over, I knew I had to put on my big girl's panty and restart my life. I can't remember spending much time wallowing or feeling sorry for myself. I didn't have the time for that. Was I hurt and mad? Heck yeah, I was. Did I ask God and the universe why? For sure I did. But I truly never spent any significant amount of time feeling sorry for myself or moping. That wasn't a choice. That just wasn't an option for me. I did not have that luxury. I had four kids who were depending on me. I had to snap out of it and get on with the business of rebuilding our lives.

# LESSONS

*"Wisdom comes with the ability to be still. Just look and just listen. No more is needed. Being still, looking, and listening activates the non-conceptual intelligence within you. Let stillness direct your words and actions."*
— *Eckhart Tolle, Stillness Speaks*

ONE VERY MEMORABLE and important moment came on my birthday that year. I turned 32. A family member called to wish me a happy birthday. We talked a few minutes and afterward, he apologized for not reaching out sooner. By then, it'd been about two months since everything started, and Robert was out of the house. I told him it was fine, and that the kids and I are doing well. Something he said at the end of the conversation stayed with me for a long time. Till today even. He said "Roxie, I want you to know something. I know you're in a lot of pain right now. I know it may feel like it's too much to handle but I want you to know that you will be fine. You will be ok. You were not born with a husband. You were fine before him, and you will be fine after him. Just remember that, and you will be fine". This resonated so much. It became my mantra. When things got tough as they often did, I'd go back to that conversation. I'd repeat it to myself again and again. "Snap out of it Roxie, you weren't born with a husband. You were fine before, you'll be fine now." Those words got me out of bed and through life again and again. I repeat them before I even start to feel bad. Because of how powerful those words were for me, I do my best to try and lift others' spirits every chance I get. It could be a perfect stranger, a friend or family. You never know when something you say will help someone, or what a difference it will make to them. No matter how insignificant we may think it is. Sometimes the smallest things make the biggest difference. I've experienced it myself many times over. Too often we don't realize the power of our words. We don't realize what powerful tools our words can be. Words can be used to break someone down or to build them up. It's up to us to decide how we use them. It's up to us to make the conscious decision to use them for good and to uplift one another.

Most recently, I have been on a spiritual journey of awakening. I have spent a great deal of time listening to the teachings of spiritual leaders such as Gary Zukav, Deepak Chopra, and Eckhart Tolle. Their teachings have made me look at life in a whole new light. I can say they have changed my life. I now understand that I am held accountable for my words and actions. Knowing the intentions behind those words and actions have consequences. Those were light bulb moments for me. To know that not only do my words and actions have consequences, but my intentions do too. Do you understand what that means? Do you see how powerful that is? Whoa!!! All we need to do is state our intentions. To be aware of those intentions, and sit back and watch the universe do its thing. In the Alchemist, Paulo Coelho says, "...And when you want something, all the universe conspires to help you achieve it". How profound is that? To know that we are not alone. That all we need is to know what we want. It is that easy. These teachings have allowed me to recognize when I am stepping out of the seat of my soul. They have taught me the importance of acting with intention. I am learning to be mindful of my thoughts. Gary Zukav teaches me to know that I am here to serve the energy of my soul, and to let the energy of my soul shine through me. Being able to recognize these things have allowed me to be more aware and conscious. Eckhart Tolle teaches me to live in the now, because everything is happening now. It's always now. I also believe that karma is real, and one way or another we pay our cosmic debts.

According to www.spiritualevolution.info- "Karma is the sum of a person's actions in this and previous lives. While on Earth, all souls live in both worlds of reincarnation and karma. Karma is justice. It does not reward or punish and shows no favoritism. The purpose of karma is to maintain balance in the Universe. In order for that balance to be maintained, living things must learn their lessons to live consciously and responsibly with a view that extends wider than just themselves. This is the path to enlightenment, and enlightenment brings greater understanding of all living and nonliving things around us."

I have had more support than imaginable. God has surrounded me with an incredible group of people. Be it friends, family, acquaintances, or even complete strangers. I do not believe in coincidences. Everything happens exactly the way they were meant to happen. Down to the exact timing of when they happen. People don't come in and out of your life haphazardly. There is a cosmic purpose behind it all. If we pay close enough attention, the reason is usually so very simple. If it's not at first, we may fight or resist, but it eventually becomes clear. We're often just too busy to see or too loud to hear. If we take the time to be still long enough it becomes clear as day. The lessons I've learned over the last decade have shaped my life today.

One of my number one rules when dealing with stress is to not sweat the small stuff. I mean they're small stuff, why sweat them? In the grand scheme of things, aren't they all small stuff? Why do we make ourselves crazy trying to make this person like us, or that person appreciate us? It took me a while to get this, and it's something I still work on. I am good enough. If I'm not good enough for you,

I'm just not your cup of tea, and that's ok. We don't all have the same tastes and flavors so go on, and find yours. Please leave the door open for the one who's been searching for mine.

# THE QUIET HOUSE

*"The laughter of the child is the light of the home"*
*— Unknown*

ONE OF THE hardest part at the beginning of all this, was the kids leaving to go spend the night with him. It was the hardest thing to wrap my mind around. It was hard enough to think of him taking the big kids, but he wanted to take Sebastian too. My newborn baby. That was a no no. He is not even one month old I would argue. What kind of a monster takes a newborn from his mother? How does he figure he can just take them like that? Even for one night. I was ready to fight for that one. He eventually saw reason and agreed to sleep on the couch downstairs with the baby in the playpen until I was comfortable with him leaving. By the time Sebastian was about three months old, he started taking him for the night with the other kids to his parents' house where he had moved.

Once he started taking the kids the house became quiet, too quiet. It went from having 3 kids and a baby running around and screaming like banshees to crickets. Those were the times that were the most unbearable. Sometimes I'd just leave. It was too hard to be there without them. It wasn't a home all alone without them. It was just a big empty house without the kids there. Those were the times that if it weren't for God, my school work and some close friends and family I could have fallen into the abyss of self-pity and sorrow. When I was alone at the house, I would go around every room turning on the TVs and radios just to have a little bit of noise. At least with that, it felt a little less lonely. I threw myself into my studies and got lost in the world of anatomy and physiology and pushed on towards my endgame.

# HAPPY HOUR AT *THE SPOT*

*"Laissez les bons temps rouler"*

THE STORY WOULDN'T be accurate without giving a nod to *The Spot*. Located in the middle of the suburbs of Naples, FL, The Spot was quite the popular bar and lounge for happy hour and the nightlife was great. It was there I would let my hair down to blow off some steam. It was there I would go and let loose the weekends the kids were with him. Heck, there were a few nights I'd be there during my time with the kids once I'd found a sitter. At *The Spot*, I wasn't some used goods somebody had cast aside. I wasn't anybody's mother. I was a woman. A woman who men still found desirable. I would have my free drinks, get my flirt on, hang with my girls, dance all night, and go back to my life. I met Al at *The Spot*. A Bahamian banker. He was Mr. tall, dark and handsome. A great kisser too. We met one night, and after dancing for hours, we later exchanged numbers. We may have spoken a handful of times and saw each other 2 maybe 3 times, but it was always at *The Spot*. He was one of those guys who showed just enough interest to keep you on the hook. Nothing ever came of Al and I other than one or two stolen kisses in the parking lot at the end of the night.

He could have definitely been a contender, but at the end of the day things just fizzled out. *The Spot* was center stage for my girls and I to let our hair down. We went by the First Wives Club, FWC for short. The name was appropriate since we were all first wives who were all either divorced, or in the process of getting divorced. The group consisted of some of my closest friends. Me, Tanya, whom I've known since elementary school. Eve whom I've known since high school, Bertina was an acquaintance I met through Eve, and my cousin/best friend Martina. We would meet there for happy hour on Friday nights, and we were there some Saturdays too if we could help it. Those nights there were all ours. We partied hard. I can only speak for myself, but those were the good old days. The proof is all over myspace. Another product of my time at *The Spot* was a relationship that went on for about two years. This was my first post-divorce relationship. He was nine years younger than me and it showed. He was a charmer, and liar all in one. That relationship lasted well past its expiration date. FWC slowly died out, though on the surface we remained friends. We still hung out, saw each other at get togethers, but as time went on, some of us just slowly got out of the party scene.

# THE RECONCILIATION

*"Reunion after long separation is even*
*better than one's wedding night."*
— *Chinese Proverb*

I T'S DECEMBER 2006. It's been five months since
he moved out. I'm in school, still living in the house,
the kids are going back and forth between him and me, and
I'm just trying to keep my head up. I met a new guy around
Thanksgiving. We had been talking since, and he invites
me to his place for the first time. This is the first person I'm
really dealing with since the separation. At least the first one
I've been intimate with. Being the chicken that I am, I call
my cousin Martina. "Hey" I say, "I'm going to that guy's
house for the first time, I'm texting you the address in case
I come up missing," I say half-jokingly. To be clear, she's the
only one I gave this information to. Not to say there was
no one else I could have told, but in the words of Meredith
Grey, Martina was my person, so it made perfect sense. I go
meet Mr. Feelgood and he starts doing his job, making me
feel good. Then my phone starts to ring. It was Robert. I
ignored it because I mean, I'm a little busy right now. Then
Martina called. Weird. She knows where I am. I'll call her

when I leave. Then it continued. Him, then her and back and forth they went. Well, there goes that I thought. My Groove is all messed up now. All sorts of crazy thoughts start going through my mind though. Are the kids ok? Does he know where I am? No, of course, he doesn't. Stop being paranoid. You have nothing to be paranoid about. You're separated and almost divorced. So I stop to internal dialog and call Martina back first.

"Girl, what's going on? Why are you and Robert blowing me up?" Are the kids ok?" I ask freaking out. "They're fine," she says sounding weird. "Robert called me" she continued. "He's asking where you are." "You didn't tell him where I am Martina, did you? He's been blowing me up". I say still freaking out. "No I didn't but he knows I'm hiding something," she says. "He says he has a feeling that someone's been in his garden" she continues. "What Garden?" I ask confused. "You" she snapped "Negro please," I said sucking my teeth, and roll my eyes Haitian style. "How would he know that Martina?" I ask. "I don't know, that's why I've been calling you" she says. "Shit!" I managed. "Ok, I'll call him. I'll call you back." Preparing myself, I call him. He answers crying. "Roxie where are you? I need to see you. I need to talk to you" "What? Why? What's wrong? Are the kids ok?" "Yes the kids are fine. I need to see you." He's practically hyperventilating on the phone. "Are you ok? Do you have your inhaler? Are you driving?" I ask worried about his asthma. "I just need to see you" he answers. "Can you meet me at the house?" He asks. "You shouldn't be driving the way you sound right now Robert. You should pull over and we can keep talking on the phone." I say. "No I need to see you, just meet me at the house" he says between sobs. "Ok" I say. "Where are the kids? Are they with you?" "No" he says, "they're with my parents.' "Ok. I'm on my way back to the house, I'll be there in about 20 minutes."

I get to the house and his car is in the driveway. I park in the garage and enter through the garage door near the laundry room. The house is dark, and I head towards the front door to turn the light on. "Roxie, I'm sorry," he says from the couch startling me. I can't see him in the dark, but I know the direction his voice is coming from. The only thing that came to my mind at that moment was this mofo is going to pull an OJ Simpson on me right here in the dark and I'm never seeing my babies again. I turn to him with the lights off and ask him what's going on. I realized I didn't turn the light on while walking to him. I changed course to head to the kitchen to turn the light on and he stops me by the stairs. He falls to his knees and hugs my legs wrapping his arms around my thighs like a 3-year-old. He's crying. What. The. Fuck. I don't even understand what's going on. He has tears, snots, and everything. All I can make out is I'm sorry, I want us to try again. I should never have left. I'd be lying if I said I remembered everything he said at the moment. I'm just freaking out because here I am, coming from another man's house. This man, my husband who I never stopped wanting. The same one who left me 5 months ago because I wasn't good enough. The one I'm in heated arguments with almost daily is on his knees in front of me asking to come home. I never asked you to leave I wanted to scream. You left me. You stopped wanting me. Yes, come home, yes come back. But I couldn't say any of those things. I'm still in shock. Still trying to process it all. Is he trying to trick me so I tell him about Mr. Feelgood? The whole time he's talking but I'm only hearing part of what he's saying. I jump when I feel him trying to take off my pants. Oh heck no, I think. I still have this other man's scent on me. I need to go take a shower I think. "Robert stop" I manage. "What's going on? What happened? I need to go take a shower. I have Sammara's holiday party to head to. I have to start getting ready." "Can I go with you?" he asks. "Go where? To the party? Robert everyone knows we're getting a divorce. How is it going to look if I walk in there with you? There'll be too many questions." "I want to come," he says. "We can talk there". I'm confused as heck, but I say ok. "I'll leave the kids with my parents but will bring the baby," he says. He leaves, and I head upstairs to shower, wondering WTF just happened.

I get ready for the party and I get on the phone with Martina. Not sure who called who, but I start telling her what's happening. She's as shocked as I am. Neither of us know what to make of the situation. I tell her I agreed for him to come to the party so we could talk. She remains adamant that she never told him about my meeting Mr. Feelgood. Robert and I arrive at the party at around the same time. We chat a few minutes outside after parking the cars. Me, in my 1999 Ford Explorer, him in his 2000 Lexus GS 350. We walk in together, inevitably get the expected looks from our friends. This was a party by one of my book club sisters, which consisted of a different group of friends. All I can do is give the Kanye shrug cause heck, I have no clue either. I vaguely remember the details of the party, but we sat together and he was very attentive. He got my drinks, fixed me a plate, we talked and played with the baby. At one point he asked, "so are we still on for tomorrow?" He must have noticed the confused look on my face cause he continued with, "our date remember?" "What date?" I asked. We agreed to go on a date tomorrow since we're not having the party". I think I laughed at the absurdity of it. "Robert we didn't agree to anything like that." We laughed about it, but he insisted. The party ended and he asked if he could come back to the house so we could keep talking. I hungrily agreed wanting more, and he followed me home.

Once home, we put the baby to bed and went to the bedroom. We sat in bed and talked all night. We planned a date for that night which he'd apparently spent time thinking about. We talked about everything. He told me about the women he dated, I told him about guys I talked to. I even told him about Al, my tall dark, and handsome Bahamian banker. It was good to be able to talk to him freely again. I didn't hesitate to tell him anything, and it felt good. We talked about getting back together but not to stop the divorce. We decided to continue with the divorce and to start dating each other. We wouldn't say anything to the kids so not to get their hopes high. Shoot, I was afraid to get my hopes high but there I was doing it anyway. We talked about how crazy we would sound to our friends and family once they found out. That was a great night. Having each other back and appreciating the second chance we were both giving our little family. My husband was back and he still loved me. I was sharing everything with him. There was so much to share with him. So much had happened over the last 5 months. It had been so long since we'd done that. We'd become enemies of sorts over the last 5 months. We had become people who lived separate lives and no longer looked out for one another. We eventually drifted to sleep right before the sun came up. When I woke up, he'd made breakfast. I didn't think there was anything else we could talk about but I was wrong. We'd been given a stay of execution so we were over the moon. He gave me some vague details about the upcoming date and since I didn't have the kids all I had to do was get myself ready.

He picked me up at the house later that night. He had roses and a bottle of champagne to celebrate. I put the flowers in water while he opened the bottle. We each had a glass before leaving. He'd manage to have the owner of a local Haitian restaurant close off the small dining area for our dining pleasure. It was nice and romantic. In an instant, I was that 19-year-old girl again, madly in love with her man. We even made it to *The Spot* that night, and ran into Bertina and her boyfriend. We drank, danced and took the rest of the celebration back to our house. We made love until morning and laid basking in the afterglow until we fell asleep in each other's arms.

The weeks to follow were nothing less than pure marital bliss. He spent more and more time at our house. The kids observed us together but never asked if we were back together. We didn't volunteer any information. I think they were afraid of not getting the answer they so badly longed for. If I could encapsulate any period in our marriage, it would be those weeks. Not even the early days could compare. At this point in our lives we knew exactly what we had and more importantly, we knew what it was like to lose it.

# THE FINAL BREAK UP

*"If you do not change direction, you may*
*end up where you are heading".*
— *Lao Tzo*

I T'S FEBRUARY 2007, Robert and I are happily dating, but the divorce is still on track. He's spending more time at the house. The kids seem happy, and we're happy. We're talking more and spending time together. One night, Robert and I were home hanging with the kids, and Martina stops by with her kids. This was not an unusual occurrence. It was the three of us and our kids. At one point Martina suggests we go to *The Spot*. My initial reply was no because not only did I have the kids, but Robert was there and I didn't want to just leave him with the kids. Not to mention her kids were there too. Robert being who he was at the time volunteered to stay with all the kids. He insisted so we went. It wasn't a particularly great night. Music was ok, but not great. I had one drink and was ready to call it a night and head home. The entire time we were there, I really just wanted to be home with him and the kids. We get back to the house and Robert is up vigorously cleaning the kitchen. It's well after midnight at this point. I say hi to him but he's in a zone and looks quite upset. He muttered something back but kept at it. Martina and I exchanged a confused look but left it alone. She and I head to my room upstairs both wondering what's got his panties in a bunch. We're laying in my bed talking and Robert comes up picking a fight. He starts going on about Al, the Bahamian banker. Why is his name coming up right now? He's saying something about me seeing Al at *The Spot* and just random accusations. It's not true. None of it is true. Stuff I can't honestly say I remember right now. He's being jealous and for the life of me, I can't understand why. Where is all of this coming from I wondered. Martina runs out of the house pretty abruptly, leaving Robert and me to finish our argument. We go on and on, and eventually, I tell him it's best if he sleeps at his parents' because I am not in the mood for the fight he's looking for. He does as I ask leaving me asking myself once again, WTF just happened.

He returns the next morning with no explanation of what caused the change in behavior the night before. Instead, we both seem to be on the same page about cutting our losses. I realized his anger issues did not go away the months we were apart, and also understanding that I'd come to enjoy the time we spent apart. I missed him, but I'd learned a lot about myself during this time. One of the fears I had about the divorce was whether or not I could do it on my own. I learned more than anything, I could do it alone. At least for the time being. God would handle the rest. I neither wanted nor needed the added theatrics. So that day we called it quits. This time it was a mutual decision. We agreed to remain as civil as possible. We even joked about remaining friends with benefits. We loosely agreed to this, and at the end, he says, "but don't tell Martina ok. She told me I couldn't go without having sex with you. I don't want to look like a punk to her." We laughed and I casually said ok. After he left, I called Martina and told her about the breakup, and our friends with benefits deal. That arrangement never happened, and I didn't think to question it.

The divorce became final a few months later. We went to the divorce hearing in separate cars. I didn't have enough cash for parking, so he paid for it. We walked in and out holding hands. Both of us were crying while signing the papers. The judge and lawyers didn't know what to make of us. We planned on going to lunch after, but he got called back to work. A part of me at this point was hopeful that at some point maybe even years down the road we would get back together. After we both figure our shit out. We stayed friends for a while after. Then that friendship became people who merely shared kids together. By that I mean we were cordial. As time progressed it became only about the kids. We would only deal with each other if it had to do with the kids and nothing else. He became increasingly more angry and hostile towards me in a short time, and I couldn't understand why.

# MOVING OUT AGAIN AND AGAIN

*"Life is a series of natural and spontaneous changes. Don't resist them - that only creates sorrow. Let reality be reality. Let things flow naturally forward in whatever way they like."*
— *Lao Tzu*

THE HOUSE WE built only two years prior was going into foreclosure. The mortgage was not being paid. I was receiving child support at the time, so by the time the divorce became final in May of 2007, I was in the process of moving into an apartment. I had a customer service job while still taking my prerequisites for nursing school. Within a year of the divorce, any child support I was getting had stopped. My attempts at understanding why were futile. This is a man who had friends in the legal field. He was a Certified Public Accountant, he worked at one of the biggest accounting firms in Estero at the time and was able to hire a very shrewd attorney. I, on the other hand, was only able to afford an attorney by selling my wedding ring. An attorney he was always quick to remind me was inadequate. He made sure to find whatever loophole he could to exploit. He was allowed to not pay any arrears child support and no longer have to pay anymore moving forward.

I was living in an apartment complex in Bonita Springs, and 11 months into my new lease, the kids and I were evicted out of the first place we called home since the foreclosure. With the child support ending, my little customer service job wasn't enough to sustain us. Thank goodness for sisters, because mine is phenomenal. My sister Yolanda and her husband Samuel opened their home to us, and we were able to move in with them. That was a tremendous help. I was able to put away a little bit of money, and 5 months later, the kids and I moved out on our own again. My sister didn't want us to move, but we needed to. It's not easy bringing five extra people to somebody else's space. Family or not, it gets crowded. The move also was an attempt at giving my crew some semblance of having their own space again.

From there, we moved into our very first efficiency apartment. Adding the word apartment to it makes it sound a lot nicer than it was. Even the word studio isn't very accurate. An efficiency unit is a section of someone's house they've closed off to rent. It's usually a small space big enough to fit a bed, leave room for maybe a hot plate and a bathroom. The bare necessities. I would have had no problem living in an efficiency, I obviously didn't. If it had been just me, I would have been fine. Low rent, utilities paid for. I'm sold. It's just not an ideal place for a family of five. We only lasted one month in that one and that was only because I had already paid her the first month so I wasn't leaving until we used up that money. It really was just too small. We then found our second efficiency apartment not too far from the first and this one was a step up from the last one. Our "room" was now big enough to put a king size mattress on the floor that was big enough for the five of us to sleep on. We had an actual stove/range in our kitchen (which was in our bedroom but who's complaining), AND we had a bathroom that was bigger than a cruise ship's bathroom. We're moving on up baby. We thought we were doing well. That was until my friend Sasha came to visit. I'm still not sure how or why I had her come because though it was better than the first place, I wasn't exactly throwing dinner parties, but the explanation could only be that it was meant to be. At this new efficiency apartment, I was paying $600 per month. $100 more than the first. Sasha came over and she was on the verge of tears. Regardless of how many times I told her we were good. I received a call from her not too long after she left telling me that her dad has a vacant 2 bedroom duplex and The kids and I are moving in. I don't even remember her asking me. She just straight up told me. That's just who she is, and I love her for it.

After 3 months in our second efficiency apartment, we moved into Sasha's dad's 2 bedroom duplex paying $800 per month. It was more money than the last place but we also had a heck of a lot more space, thank you, Sasha. The kids were excited and that was satisfaction enough for me. They were finally getting a room with a door and closet again... whoa!! We lived there for about 2 years while I was in nursing school. When the program ended so did the money because student loans financial aid was how I was paying the bills and government assistance fed us during those times. Those were our mac and cheese and ramen noodles days.

Among the many blessings, we found after the divorce were the people who I should legally be addressing as my ex-in-laws. In my heart, however, they have never been ex anything. The relationship with my mother in law and father in law has gotten a lot stronger now that I am no longer married to their son. I always had a relationship with his sisters. Cassie the youngest won my heart from the start. She was nine when I met her brother in 1994. She was my baby then, and now as a kick-ass surgeon, we remain friends and sisters. I am so proud of her. Pascale, also a doctor was away at school in Georgia when Robert and I met, but once she was back at home, our friendship flourished, and till today we are still very close friends and sisters. His oldest sister Julianna, a urologist had just left for medical school when Robert and I met, so we didn't have the same opportunity to form as close a relationship as I had with his younger sisters. She came home often enough so that gave us the chance to get to know each other some. Though we didn't have the chance to form a very close relationship when Robert and I were married, we're a lot closer now. She was there for me through the divorce and for that I am grateful. His entire family has been beyond incredible since the divorce. They love my kids to a fault. They show me so much love and appreciation. I love them all, but my father in law is very special to me. They are very present in our lives. It was due to the tightness of those relationships that once I graduated nursing school we didn't find ourselves homeless. I say this jokingly because with the number of friends and family the kids and I have, homelessness has never been a fear of ours. My in-laws found out I had no way to continue paying the bills until I passed the boards and found work. Without hesitation, my mother in law had the kids and I move in with them and we stayed 5 months. I was able to look for work while I was there. Once I landed my first nursing job, I was able to start saving and was able to move into an apartment not too far from them. She wanted us to stay longer so I could save more, but I was grateful for the time she gave us, and it was time to start get on my own and get life started again. We lived in that apartment complex for 5 years before buying our first post-divorce home 10 ½ years after their father moved out. That was the longest we lived in one place, and it felt nice.

# THE BETRAYAL

*"Forgive them, father, for they know not what they do"*
*— Jesus H. Christ*

Y OU MIGHT WANT to take a seat, because this
may take a while.

We all come from somewhere. We all have a family. We may
not claim them all, but we have them. There's the family you
come from, and then there's the family you choose. As for me,
I've been fortunate enough to have had a good combination
of both my entire life. Coming from a big family, we have all
sorts. Good, bad or indifferent I can say there's a lot of love in
my family. We argue and fight but we never stop being family.
There's no black sheep, we have some eccentric members but
they're keepers. To really get a good understanding of the
dynamic, I have to go way back. Hope I don't lose you.

My mom, the second of 10 kids on my grandmother's side
is the ultimate giver. Eldest to her, is my sweet aunt Marie-
Lourdes who is of a different father. He had other children
among whom is my uncle Rene. He has been part of the
family before I was even a twinkle in my father's eye. Rene
has a daughter, Martina. Martina and I grew up as cousins,
though there's no real blood relations. We have pictures

together as early as three years old. I grew up in Haiti until age twelve, she was born in Boston and raised by her mom in Hawaii until the end of High School. She moved to Estero sometime in 1993 and lived on and off with my family and I. I'd graduated high school the previous year.

This is where our story truly began. We became your regular Thelma and Louise. We did everything together. Whenever I'd go on a date, which wasn't often, I'd find a way to fix her up with their brother, or friend. They were by no means pity dates, she was a beautiful girl, and quite progressive because, after all, she was from Hawaii. The dates for me never became anything serious until I met Robert the following new year. True to form, I continued setting her up with Robert's friends when he and I would go on dates. She eventually dated and married a friend I went to high school with who lived down the street from me. He saw her and fell in love with her and it was a done deal.

Martina was my cousin and best friends. She wasn't exactly blood, but she was nonetheless my family. I chose her. She chose me. That to me is a stronger bond than any blood connection. We got married around the same time, raised our children together. Our lives were pretty much one. Our kids were around the same ages. There wasn't much we didn't know about each other. Our lives revolved around each other. It wasn't just the two of us, we were a set of about five couples: Roxie and Robert, Martina and Max, Sasha and

Brad, Jim and Elizabeth, Eve and Freddy. There were more but the 10 of us did a lot together. We were inseparable. The kids would have play dates, the women hung out together, the men did their thing, we did our things as couples and as a family. Martina was very particular about me explaining our connection to people. She would lose her shit if I ever tried explaining the shared aunt connection. "People would minimize our relationship if you keep explaining it" she would say. I'd agree because regardless what anyone had to say she was my cousin. Even more than that, she was like a sister. Fast forward pass our happy days. Only two of the five couples mentioned earlier are still married. Martina and Max divorced. So did Eve and Freddy. The First Wives Club came and went. Martina started distancing herself from the group, but we still talked, just not as often. Eve and I remained close. She and I still partied, just not like it was with the FWC, but we still got our fun in.

It is early 2008, and more and more friends keep asking me "What's going on with Martina and Robert?" My answer is usually the same. "Nothing, she needs help with the kids and Robert helps her I guess, I don't know." It was just being asked more and more. I had that feeling in my core that was always heavy. Never felt right whenever someone would ask about them. By this time Martina had started to distance herself from me as well. She didn't do it right away but looking back it, It was bit by bit. By then I wasn't partying as much as

I used to. One way I can describe Martina is as a chameleon. She can be whoever you need her to be. She could be one way with one group, and completely different with another. That should have been my first clue.

One day, a friend asked me again what was up with them, and this time it stayed with me. So I gave her a call. No answer. She only lived about five minutes away so I drove to her house. My name is on her guest list so the guard naturally just lets me in. I get there and start knocking. No answer. I continue knocking, and calling. Nothing. I drive away, and by the time I get home, she's calling me. "Why were you at my house"? Was my greeting. "Why didn't you answer the door if you knew it was me?" "I didn't know who it was. I saw your car as you were leaving," she lies. "Why didn't you call sooner then?" I rebutted." Why didn't the guard call when you got here" she asks ignoring my question. "Because I'm on your guest list Martina. Remember me? Roxie, your cousin". "What do you want? Why did you come?" She interrupts, irritated. "I came to ask if you're fucking Robert," I ask bluntly. "No I'm not fucking Robert" her lies continued. "Why would you ask me that? feigning surprise. "Because people won't stop asking me about the two of you since you seem to be joined at the hip lately," I said. The conversation went on for a while. She lied and denied everything the entire time. We hang up and I cried myself to sleep knowing there was a lot more than she was telling me. That feeling in my gut just would not go away.

The next day, I was working at the girls' school. I worked as a substitute teacher around this time, and since the kids were still young, I tried to be at their school as often as possible. The class was at recess on the playground when my phone rang. It was Robert. He went in on me immediately, demanding to know why I had been at Martina's house so late last night. That was one of the most traumatizing conversations I have had with this man in all the time I'd known him. I don't remember everything about that particular conversation because, after years of playing it over and over, I locked it away in the deepest parts of my mind. The part that I do remember and will never forget is when he said "I'm in love with Martina, and we're in a relationship. I need you to stop calling and harassing her." I froze, the playground was spinning, I was outside but felt like someone put a plastic bag over my face because I couldn't breathe. Couldn't catch my breath. "Harassing?" I thought. I only questioned her once about this. I wanted to throw up. I don't think even the divorce made me feel as sick as I was feeling at that moment. What are you talking about? I was thinking. Are you talking about Martina? My Martina? Did he meet someone else name Martina? Was he talking about a different Martina?" Mwen pa compren (*I don't understand*). But he did mean my Martina. His Martina now I guess. But how? When? Why?

Why would they do that to me? Why would they hurt me like this? These are people who love me. Could they not find anyone else to be with?

I somehow made it home from subbing that day. I cried more than I cried for a while. What ensued was not my proudest moment I'll admit, but damn it, it felt good. If only momentarily. I make no excuses for it, but I have since apologized for it.

I fired up my desktop and took a seat at the computer desk in the living room of my apartment, and I start typing. I type through tears, barely able to read the computer screen but I keep typing. If she can do this to me her friend, her cousin, her sister, what won't she do to someone else? I am hurt beyond measure. I feel broken beyond repair. I'm going to let the world know who and what she really is. How could I have been so dumb as to trust her this much? How long has this been going on? Have I been blind all these years? How long had she been wanting him? How long had they been wanting each other? I'm going to be sick, but I don't stop. Martina is a very private person. She loves putting on pretenses. She'd hate more than anything to have the story be made public before she had a chance to spin it herself. Now, this was the days before Olivia Pope, but she could put Liv to shame. She did, after all, have an English degree and and was very articulate. This chick could sell ice water to Eskimos. I knew the only way to beat her at her own game was to put it out there before she could spin the story into something it was not. I needed her to feel what I am feeling. I need her to see what she did to me, to my kids. So I sent a mass email and made sure to include her and Robert. I needed them to know it came from me. I spilled my guts. I sang like a canary. If I had an email address for you at the time and you knew either party, chances are you were carbon copied. Again, not my proudest moment. Of course, this triggered an onslaught of back and forth emails among the three of us. Robert, serving as her mouthpiece did most of the talking and emailing for her. That just showed how spineless she was. The only demand I had was for her to come to me face to face. Woman to woman to tell me she was in love with Robert. My ex-husband. The father of my four children. That is one thing that never happened. She cowered behind Robert and let him fight her battles for her. Not something I could ever respect. Martina at the time was in the middle of her own divorce/ separation. A lot of the secrets I revealed that day were I'm guessing a surprise to her then-husband, whom I gladly forwarded whatever ammunition he needed for their divorce.

I later came to see there was no true satisfaction in sending that email. It was sent from a place of hurt and anger. They were still together. I was still hurt. The email didn't change that. The betrayal remained. It wasn't the right way to handle the situation. It's not who I am. It's who I was driven to be.

How could I give anyone that kind of the power over me? I've since asked God for forgiveness. It's something I take responsibility for. I now do my best not to react when I am hurt or angry. I try to take time to reflect if I am able to so that I may react more objectively. I can't say I am always successful in doing this, but as with most things, it is a work in progress. All I can say is I am better at it today than I was yesterday and hope to be even better at it tomorrow.

The two eventually married. They subjected both sets of kids to their filth. Martina who once made sure we had the kids on the same weekends managed to switch the weekends up once she alienated me and got closer to Robert. So now, she and Robert had the kids on the same weekend and were kid free at the same time. Nicely played girl, nicely played. She is now also quick to tell everyone that we are not related. She now tells anyone who will listen that we are not related by blood. That we used to be friends. Used to be huh? Girl bye!

I can't speak for her kids, but mine were miserable their entire marriage. That is putting it mildly. They were traumatized. Thank goodness the boys were too young to know something wasn't right, but my girls unfortunately by then were old enough to know what they were witnessing. I once overheard Priya talking to one of her friend's about the situation, and she said "I wonder what their answer is when people ask them about how they met." It broke my heart to know how much she thought about that situation. Martina's kids who once were their cousins are now their step-brother and step-sister. My heart went out to them because just like my kids they were innocent bystanders. Collateral damage.

They have since divorced, thank the Lord. I can't for the life of me figure out how those two thought they could make this work. How could they think they could find love, peace and happiness from causing so much pain and anguish. Their actions did not only hurt and affected me. It hurt and affected my kids and her kids. It hurt and affected his relationship with his family. I can say the biggest loss for me from all of this was losing Martina. A lot more so than Robert. My relationship with her is what I mourned every single time I think about this. Here is someone I loved and trusted blindly. I mean blindly. Never in a million years would I expect this level of betrayal from her. She's the person I would run to when something big happened to me. This was something big. She is the one I'm supposed to run to with this. She's the one I'm supposed to call and say let's go kick this bitch's ass. How does that work now? I was angry at her for taking that away from me. For breaking what we had for something that didn't last. Something that didn't even last. Was it worth it? Would you do it again given the chance? How did you let it get this far? How did it begin in the first place?

# FORGIVING

*"We must develop and maintain the capacity to*
*forgive. He who is devoid of the power to forgive is*
*devoid of the power to love. There is some good in the*
*worst of us, and some evil in the best of us. When we*
*discover this, we are less prone to hate our enemies"*
*— Dr. Martin Luther King Jr.*

I USED TO ALWAYS hear that forgiveness isn't for the other person, it's for you. I didn't get it until I got it. One of my favorite quotes says *"Holding on to anger is like drinking poison and expecting the other person to die" -Unknown.* There is so much truth to that, and I lived and experienced it. I was hurt and angry for so long. It was killing me. Even when I'd think I was ok and dealt with it, all it took was for one person to mention their names in the same sentence to set me off. It took two separate occasions, years apart for me to finally break free of the Martina and Robert shackles.

The first occurred in church. This particular Sunday morning, the sermon was about, you guessed it, forgiveness. I didn't think too deeply about it, because after all, this thing was old news. Well, little did I know God was using this service to free my heart. The ushers passed around a tray of seashells. It became what I later saw a reverse offering. From Him to me. The idea was to focus on any anger, pain or hurt we're feeling and to release it onto that seashell. After that, we were to throw that shell away along with our pain, hurt and anger. Well, as I sat there in the pew of my local non-denominational church, I reached for a shell out of the basket as it was passed to me. I sat there listening to instructions by the preacher. I closed my eyes and thought of the two of them. I let my body relax as I felt its need to tense up as these memories came up like a surge. I remembered the love I had for the two of them. The love despite myself I still had for them both. Robert, I thought is the father of my babies. He is a person that will be in my life for as long as the kids are alive and as long as they have children and their children have children. My kids are half him. How do I hate him without hating half of my children? Whatever his motivation for starting this relationship is his and not for me to understand. It must have filled some need for them. This is a situation I have absolutely no control over. How is remaining angry and bitter going to change the situation? How does that help my children? Forgive him, Roxie, I felt a warm and soothing feeling working its way up from my core to exit as a cleansing breath, and I exhaled. Martina, I thought for now is a part of him which makes her part of them for as long as they remain on this path. Forgive Roxie! You love her, Pray for her. Let it go. I exhaled another cleansing breath and focused it all

ROXIE GAULTIER

on the seashell. I practiced this a few times and felt lighter. I knew this was something I would have to practice regularly. Something I would have to mindfully work on in order to get better at it.

The second occurred during a Reiki circle years later. I had no idea what Reiki was before my then Polish boyfriend introduced me to it. He himself is a Reiki master. He explained it, and eventually took me to my very first Reiki circle. It was held in a crystal shop somewhere in East Naples. He explained to me what was going to happen but it still didn't prepare me for what I was about to experience. We sat in a circle and it started with guided meditation. We were instructed to imagine standing in front of a lake, and in the very center of that lake was the person we need to forgive. That person could be yourself or someone else. I didn't have two people in that lake, just one and her name is Martina. There she was standing there in my mind. The person leading the meditation continues with the instructions. Continue to the center of the lake. Look them in the eye he instructs. Tell them you forgive them. Release them of any wrongdoing he says. As I'm receiving these instructions, I begin to experience the same warm sensation I did a couple of years ago in that church. I continued releasing her from the responsibility for the pain and hurt. You're not responsible for that Martina, only I am. I own the pain hurt and anger now. I release you from it all. I forgive you. Our final instruction was to submerge ourselves in the water leaving behind any negative feeling associated with the person or situation, and I did. I walked out of that lake, and when we were guided out of the meditation to say I felt better or lighter would be inaccurate, What I felt was a sense of ease, and calmness that has since stayed with me.

# THE CALL

*"When I let go of what I am, I become what I might be.*
*When I let go of what I have, I receive what I need."*
— *Lao Tzu*

IT'S OCTOBER 2017. I am working in San Francisco, CA, but staying in Napa Valley. The commute is long and I am working nights. Needless to say, sleep is even more important than usual. It's the middle of the day, and I should be asleep for work but for some reason I am awake. I'm in my hotel room bed trying to will myself back to sleep when my cell rings. The number is not in my contacts, but it could be a job, so I answer. "Hello," I say trying to sound fully awake. "Roxie?" asks a voice I don't recognize right away. "Yes", I reply. "It's Martina," she says. I literally took the phone away from my ear to look at it cause I'm in the twilight zone right now. As I placed the phone back to my ear I hear, "yes I know it's Martina." I always thought if that day ever came, I knew exactly what I'd say to her. Truth be told I had no clue what to say. Here it is almost 10 years later. I was speechless. I think my first reply was something like. Oookkk? As I start looking around the room for what, I don't know. Then she starts. "This is a call I should have made a long time ago. I tried calling before but Robert wouldn't allow me to." Allow you to? I thought. She continued without stopping. "I'm calling to apologize and I don't know, reconcile." Reconcile? I thought. Is that what she just said? "What I did to you was unforgivable. I was wrong. It was wrong. I should never have married your ex-husband. I want to apologize." I lost it at that moment. "Why are you doing this Martina?" I shout, now in tears. I can barely hear my own voice above my sobs. "Why are you doing this now?" "I know Roxie, and I'm sorry. It's something that I have to do. I should have done it years ago. I'm sorry it's taken so long for me to do it." Her apologies felt sugar-coated for her own sake. Though I was not expecting her call, I'm glad she called. That call, however, wasn't for me. It was for her. She asked for forgiveness but that was something I had done years ago. Something I released the both of them of in order for me to be ok. It was nice to hear her acknowledge her part in it, but the actual act of forgiving I had done long ago. I explained that much to her. The conversation in all lasted one hour, one minute, twenty-three seconds. It went from her apologizing, to me breaking down all the hurt her actions caused. I told her of the venom that Robert now has for me, all because their relationship wasn't accepted by his family. A relationship that had a zero chance of survival. I told her of the fracture it caused in so many aspects of our lives. How their relationship affected my kids, and their relationship with their father. She would accept none of it. That wasn't for me force her to accept it. This was our first opportunity to have an actual conversation. I wasn't interested in shaming her, but since she called I had questions to ask and things I wanted to bring to her attention that she may have closed her eyes to. There wasn't anything I particularly NEEDED from her. So I didn't do a lot of pushing. It felt odd talking to her for that long though. It was something we hadn't done in over ten years. I didn't expect to do that ever again. Someone I used to talk to all day every day, now a complete stranger. There was nowhere else to take the conversation, so we eventually said our goodbyes and hung up. I found myself laying flat on my back on the hotel bed looking up at the ceiling thinking WTF just happened.

I spent a good amount of time reflecting on that call days later. Even text her for clarification. I thought of all the things I could have said, all the things I should have said. I decided I said all that I needed to say and she did as well. I had to remind myself the call was for her and not me. Up to now I only told a handful of people about the call. I never even told Robert. What would be the point? Five years ago I would have taken an ad out in the paper to announce it. Telling the world you see… I was right. Even she knows she was wrong. Now don't get me wrong. Nothing about what went down with them was right. I just no longer had the need to feel vindicated. God freed me from it all years ago and that is the best feeling in the world.

I've prayed for her regularly from the start. I pray for her and her kids. I prayed for her and Robert when they were together. This isn't something a lot of people understand. This woman was an intricate part of my life. She was for a time living with my children half of the time. She had access to their food, had access to them while they slept, when they were most vulnerable. What else was there for me to do other than to wish her well? Other than to pray that God touches her heart so she treats my children well. When everything came out, she confessed to members of the family that she was jealous of me and my marriage. Of the way Robert loved me. Robert is many things, but one thing I can say about him is he loves his children. He doted on them. Who knows how her jealousy would manifest toward them if she felt Robert was giving them more love than her? So yes, I prayed for her. Now that she's no longer with him, I still pray for her. I pray she finds what she's looking for. I pray for her kids whom I love dearly. There's no room in my life or heart for hate. I adopted this quickly after I realized the hurt would consume me if I didn't channel it properly, so I did.

# MY CALLING

*"As a nurse, we have the opportunity to heal the heart,*
*mind, soul, and body of our Patients, their families*
*and ourselves. They may forget your name, but they*
*will never forget how you made them feel."*
— *Maya Angelou*

NURSING SCHOOL WAS something my mom tried to push me to do since I graduated high school in 1992. Even now I look back on it, and I ask myself "why didn't you do it then?" The answer is always the same. It wasn't the time. I started my nursing path immediately after he left the house. Those classes were not easy or cheap. I wasn't receiving any financial aid yet, but I managed to pay for classes. Now there was a matter of my books. I remember Eve called me one day to go to Target with her. I wasn't especially busy so I met her there. We're walking around the store talking. She stops, takes my hand and put something in my palm and closes it. "For your books," she said. I looked down and there was all this money. I didn't know how much it was yet but it was enough to make me cry. It was $300 in cash. That was just one of the many times she was there for me. I hugged her tight. Thank you seemed insufficient. More on that friendship later.

If I thought prerequisites were tough, nursing school was no joke. The saying was "C" your way through it". That's what most of us did. I don't care if you came in with a 5.0 GPA, this program was bound to knock you down a notch or two. It was one of the hardest things I've done in my life. In our very first lecture, my favorite professor, Dr. Tranell warned us. This program is not for everyone, and she was not lying. When I started nursing school I was working my customer service job, and had a boyfriend. He was more like my fifth child really. Trying to juggle nursing school, the kids, work, and a boyfriend wasn't the best idea. At first, I was killing it. When everyone else was struggling, I was getting Bs. I was thinking, what's everyone talking about? I got this. Then the second half of the semester came and I wasn't feeling so confident. First thing I had to let go of was the boyfriend. He was a distraction I did not need, not to mention he wasn't bringing anything extra to my life other than some good sex. He probably lasted as long as he did because of the sex. By the end of the second half of the semester, my Bs had all disappeared, and I failed Nursing Process 2 and pharmacology. Well, that just won't do. I am getting this nursing license come hell or high water. Something had to give, and that something was work. That was a decision I struggled with. I'm not getting any child support, no alimony at that point. If I stop working how am I supposed to feed the kids? How will I pay the bills? Sometimes I falter and forget who my God is. After praying immensely on it, I decided God did not bring us this far to leave us, so decision made. I quit my job. Now what? Thanks to President Obama, there was ample money for school. They even had single parents money, that's me! I applied for all the scholarships I qualified for, student loans, financial aid you name it. The best part is I got most of it. With that, I had to focus on the necessary remediation to get back on track. After sitting out for a semester I was back. I was determined to get to the finish line and finish I did. What a feeling that was, but that was only half the battle. I still had to take the boards.

If you are a recluse, nursing school is not for you. I would never dream of telling anyone what career path to take. I say this because this is a program you cannot survive alone. You have to make friends, they don't start out as friends. They're connections and study buddies. They become the only people in your life for the time being who understand your plight. You have a shared stressor, and that's when the friendship and comradery are born.

Candle lighting was on August 1st, 2010. Everyone came out to support. My entire family, near and far. My in-laws, friends. Everyone was there. I felt the love. They even managed to throw me a surprise party. I am not the easiest person to surprise, so kudos to them for managing to pull it off without giving anything away. Once graduation was over, I was on a mission to not do anything having to do with school. I did not touch a single book until the kids started school at the end of the month. This was my time to chill and do nothing. I hung out with my friends, and binged watched shows on Netflix. Finally the kids were back in school. That's when I finally picked up the books again. I would drop them off at school in the morning, and head to the library to study. I'd leave to pick them up when school let out, and do NCLEX practice questions at night. That was my routine for two weeks.

Finally the day came. I was tired of studying. If I don't know it by now, I ain't gonna know it. All the necessary paperwork was in, all fees were paid, and it was time to take the NCLEX -RN. I told no one I was going, I just went. It was the day of my 36th birthday. This would either be a good thing or a very bad thing, but I was optimistic. The test didn't feel as hard as I was expecting it to and that worried me. It took two hours. The computer shut off after 75 questions and I froze. OMG! This could be good, or it could be bad. Shit! I look at the facilitator, and she motions for me to go to her. I kept telling myself, Roxie this is normal, you did well. She gave nothing away. Bella, a dear friend I met in A&P who has since become like a sister called to wish me a happy birthday. She'd passed her boards a year before me and was already working as a nurse. I couldn't hold it anymore, "I just took the NCLEX" I blurted. She was excited for me, reassure me I did well. I told her I had no clue how I did, but it was out of my hands. Now we wait for 24 hours. I headed to Marco Island for breakfast, and to walk on the beach and clear my mind. The next day I woke up bright and early to check my score. Nothing. Sebastian, now four years old woke up with what looked like the pink eye. Poor baby could not even open his eyes pass a certain point. I dropped the big kids off at school and we headed to Dr. Smith, the Pediatrician. We're early so the office is still closed. We sit on the bench outside waiting. I'm not giving up on searching for my score. With Sebastian next to me on the bench, my Blackberry in my hand I'm scrolling through the board of nursing website on the tiny screen. I must have refreshed a thousand times. Then, while scrolling I see the words LICENSE NUMBER with actual numbers next to the words, and the numbers started with the letters RN. I screamed, startling Sebastian. "Mommy are you ok? What's wrong he asked?" "I passed my test baby. Mommy passed her test." I was crying, jumping and hugging him now. "Did you get an A?" he asked beaming for me. "Mommy got an A baby. Mommy got an A"

My uncle had a nurse friend working at a nursing home in Lehigh and arranged for me to get an interview. It was short and sweet and I was hired on the spot. I couldn't believe it. My very first nursing job. The pay was good, the distance wasn't ideal, but heck, I was about to be an employed nurse, you couldn't tell me nothing. I easily fell into my role as a nurse albeit a nursing home wasn't the ideal job I envisioned in nursing school, I now had the chance to work with one of my favorite groups, the elderly. It was beautiful. Then I received my first check. What a thing of beauty that thing was. All those years of studying and lack of sleep was finally paying off. I was actually earning a living for my babies. I could now take care of them, feed all on my own. That check in my hand was proof of that. I didn't even want to cash it.

I became a travel nurse in November 2012. I did not set out to be a travel nurse. It wasn't something on my radar. I'd heard about travel nursing, so it's something I had in the back of my mind to start doing once the kids were older. My career as a travel nurse was born out of necessity. I was constantly getting canceled at my job at Doctors Regional in Naples where I worked. It became so bad that even as a full-time employee we would sometimes work one day per week instead of the typical three. For a single mom of four in a single income household, that just wouldn't do. I was surfing nursing jobs online, and one day I received a call with an offer to work in Arizona. I'm not sure why I even entertained the idea, but I did. I called my mother in law and told her about it. She is also a nurse and understood the struggle. Without hesitation, she said, "Go, leave the kids with me and go". I was like, "it's an eight-week contract mommy." So? She rebutted "I'll keep them for 8 weeks. Go. Robert will take them on his weekend, and they'll be at my house on your time." This is the mother of my ex-husband. This woman never ceases to amaze me. Just like that, I became a travel nurse, and the rest is history.

Nursing I soon came to realize was never a job for me, it's so much more. It truly was my calling. I absolutely love what I do. I love taking care of my patients. Watching them slowly improve. That brings me so much joy and satisfaction. To be that shoulder for a family member who just lost a loved one. Holding the hand of the patient who is scared. The simple act of sitting at a patient's bedside and letting them talk. We don't always have the luxury of sitting down to simply listen, but when you can, you do. Those are all priceless moments for me. The fact that something I love to do so much gives me a paycheck at the end of the day, well that's just nuts. Sometimes it blows my mind that I get paid to do it.

As with all great things, the profession has its pluses and minuses. There have been days I come home and can't even get out of my car from being so tired. Working 4-5 straight 12 hour night shifts eventually take its toll. There are also other aspects to the job. There are those pesky red tapes and politics that comes with the job. Why can't I just show up, take care of my patients, and go home? That would be oh so sweet. There's also patient ratio to consider, safe and good working conditions. Good bad or indifferent, I am blessed to be a part of this wonderful club of lifesavers.

# STUCK IN THE MIDDLE

*"We must take sides. Neutrality helps
the oppressor, never the victim.
Silence encourages the tormentor, never the tormented."*
— *Elie Wiesel*

IT STARTED IN the fall of 1991. I am starting my senior year in high school, and she is an incoming sophomore. We met in the cafeteria. She needed directions which I happily provided. We were both Haitian, and she seemed nice enough. To top it off, she turned out to be my then boyfriend Trevor's cousin so that sealed the deal. We became immediate friends. Our friendship was born in high school, but we didn't become BFFs until after she graduated a few years later.

It was 1995 when we finally truly reconnected. I knew she didn't leave the state for college because we would see each other around town. I knew that she stayed with her high school sweetheart Freddy cause those two were as bad as Trevor and I were with the kissing and making out in the hallways. With everything unfolding in my life at the time, we were not in touch all the time. One day, in the second trimester of my pregnancy with Priya, I pulled up to the resident's lane of the guards' gate at our apartment complex. I happened to look to my left and there is Pierre, Freddy's older brother who graduated the same year as me. "What's up stranger?" I say as I poke my head out of the driver side window. "Hey Roxie" he replies surprised to see me. "What are you doing here?" He asks. "I live here" I say, "what are you doing here?" "Freddy and Eve live here" he tells me. "What?? Are you kidding me?" I shout. "You're lying." "No" he laughs, and the cars behind us start honking at us. "I'm visiting them now, you should come up with me" he says. "Heck ya" I say, and follow behind him. We hug saying hello and head toward the elevator. I waddle behind him rubbing my belly. We agree to surprise them, so I peak my head in the doorway followed by my enormous belly, after Pierre is greeted by a very pregnant Eve. We both scream, elated as we register the fact that we're both pregnant. We hug and jump and squeal like seven year old little girls. I visit with them for what seemed like hours trying to catch up on what's been going on with each other. We're surprised to find out we got married two weeks apart and our due dates are only a little over two weeks apart. I'm having a girl and she a boy, Tony. We're just so happy to see each other. My apartment was in the next building over. I tell her about my husband and I can't wait for them to meet him. Once they met, Robert and Freddie became fast friends. Robert later became the godfather of their last son Rick.

From this point on we became inseparable. She was my boo. I delivered three weeks early and she had Tony two days after my delivery. I remember wheeling Priya's baby carriage to her hospital room to meet her Tati Eve the day after she was born. We couldn't believe that we were both there at the same time. I went on to have three more kids and she had two more. Indya is two months older than her second son Jerry, and my Quincy is two month older than her son Rick. It was beyond crazy. Everyone thought we planned it each time. How can you plan these things? We weren't exactly synchronizing our ovulation dates or our love making sessions. We did have fun telling people the stories though. It was all too funny. Unreal even. Nobody believed us, but we didn't care. In fact our other friends all had kids around the same time too. I seemed to be the ringleader since all my kids were the first to be born in the bunch. I wish I had that kind of power i would joke. The good thing is though the kids all grew up together and were never bored, cause they always had each other. Martina's kids were the same ages, so were Sasha and Brad's as well as Jim and Elizabeth's. We were all one big happy family.

Surprisingly enough Eve, Martina and I started going through the divorce process at around the same time. One after the other. Now fast forward past my divorce and the betrayal. Eve and Freddie were the only ones out of our close circle of friends who remained friends with Martina and

Robert. Freddie, I didn't expect to change, but Eve was a surprise to me. It was never something I understood, but I kept quiet about it for years as I tried to not let it affect me. It eventually did and I said something about it. She explained to me that Robert is the godfather of her son and a good friend. In her book he is a good person who did a bad thing and she doesn't think she should stop talking to him for that. She insisted that she is choosing to remain neutral. Not exactly the response I was expecting from my BFF, but I accepted it. I tried to understand. I knew she loved me. I knew she wasn't remaining friends with them out of malice, but it still hurt. That's just who she is. My wanting things to be different wouldn't make them so.

We continued our post-divorce lives dating, partying it, and planning activities with the kids on our weekends with them. It started becoming harder and harder to accept her straddling the fence on the issue. As much as I tried, it kept bugging me. I once more addressed the issue with her, but was determined to not have it be an ultimatum. If there's something I strongly dislike it is an ultimatum. All it does is force someone to choose you over someone or something else. For me, if you choose me it's because you want to, not because you didn't have a better option. So when I approached her, it was basically to let her know that, I could no longer look at pictures of her at a dining room table breaking bread with people who do not wish me well. People who hated me.

Right or wrong it was how I felt and still feel. It may have been selfish on my part, but it's the way it makes me feel. I wasn't comfortable with her knowing all my little secrets and still be as close to them as she was. I'm not sure I was ever afraid of her telling them anything. That isn't who she is. It's not something she would do. She said she's close to Robert, but not Martina but she accepts his life as it is. I told her I have no choice to accept what she's telling me, however I am choosing to remove myself from the equation. My feelings on the issue at the time was this. Martina and Robert both chose each other. Here Eve was choosing them or at least choosing Robert. At which point was somebody going to chose me? My decision at the time was simple. I chose me. That's all it came down to. Me choosing myself. I did not want or need to explain that to anyone.

Three months later, I received a text from her at 630am telling me she was in my driveway. I told her to come in. She had been clubbing the night before and drove to my house instead of going home. She spent a while debating if she should message me. I'm glad she did. We laid in my bed talking for hours, dozed off and talked some more. I had missed her so much, and she felt the same. We didn't address the elephant in the room but we picked up right where we left off friendship wise. Our lives went on, and we were back to being thick as thieves and ever so involved in one another's lives.

We're both nurses. She was my guiding light going into the nursing program. She pushed and encouraged me and was there for me through it all. She was front and center at candle lighting and we celebrated accordingly. I love this woman. Once I started working, we would talk on our drive to and from working being that we both work nights. We never went a day without talking to each other. She tried to keep her friendship with Robert separate as best she could. We had a spot on the beach where we practically lived. Our times off work and without the kids were spent there just chilling and enjoying the our beautiful state.

It's February 2012, I am in bed sleeping after work when I receive a call from Indya at school telling me she is now a 'woman'. Both extremely excited and sleepy I get out of bed and create a little package for her with all the essentials. It was a Thursday. They go to their dad every Thursday so I knew I wouldn't be seeing her until the next day. I head to her school to hug and kiss and welcome her to womanhood. She was happy but a little shy and embarrassed at the same time. I told her we would celebrate properly when she got back to me the next day. I gave her the little package I prepared for her and sent her back to class with more hugs and kisses.

I had already told Robert before heading to the school. On my way home, I called my sister, my mom, mother in-law and one of Robert's sisters. I figured I'll tell anyone else who needed to know eventually. This is a big deal in the Haitian community. It's a right of passage everywhere but we tend to make big announcements on the subject. I hated it when my mom did it to me, but there I was doing it. Sorry baby girl. I thought about calling Eve, but I figured I would either tell on our drive to work later or chances are, Robert would no doubt tell her. I was tired and ready to go back to sleep.

Driving to work that night I called Eve as usual. She answers with "I heard about some big news today that I thought I would have heard from my BFF". "I know" I replied. "I'm sorry. I was so tired girl, I had to wake up to go to the school so I just went back to sleep once I got back home. I figured if Robert didn't tell you about it, we'd talk about it on the drive to work." I said. "Suuure," she replies not convinced" "Seriously," I said. Then we fell into conversation about how time flies, and recalling our pregnancy days with Indya and Jerry, and now she is a "woman". We laughed about how silly that sounded. Then I said, "Well it sucks I'm working tonight, and have to wait till tomorrow to have a nice mother daughter talk with her. Robert better not have his chick have any sort of talk with my baby. She needs to know her place." At this Eve became quiet. "You know she's helping him raise the kids right? She is their stepmother so I'm sure he'll have her to talk to her." Mind you I am on I-75, a major highway and I see red. This is my best friend, she knows the situation. How could this be her reply to me? Keeping calm, I say "I know who she is Eve. She has a daughter of her own who will one day have her own right of passage. She'll have a chance to have that talk too. Today though is my daughter's turn. Her mother is alive and well and is well equipped to talk to her, so no that is not her place. She can congratulate her, but there will be no sit down sort of talk going on in that house tonight. Robert knows better." Her next reply floored me. I don't know how I kept driving straight. "You know he's not coming back right Roxie?" He's with her and they are living their lives and raising the kids is part of it." I'm not sure how long it took me to get to work from that point or how I even got there. "Why do you always feel the need to defend them?" This isn't an issue of me wanting him back. It's about her know her place. I'm almost screaming. I'm hot now. "I'm not defending them. I'm trying to make you see reason" she says. We eventually hang up. I sat in the car feeling hurt and crush. I cried for five to ten minutes not believing the conversation I just had. All I'm thinking is WTF just happened? I regained my composure, found the closest bathroom to wash my face and get my shift started. We would typically text and chat during the night if we had the chance but that did not happen. I drove home in silence the next morning instead of being immersed in our usual ride home conversations. By the time I reached home, I received what I can only refer to as a ten page letter (via text) from her reiterating her point from the night before. As if she didn't drive the knife deep enough, she was giving it one last twist for good measure. I closed the text, and cried myself to sleep knowing we'd reached the end of the road.

For the next three months I thought of nothing else. I did not want to rush to judgement. I looked at it from all sides. Hers and mine. Even Robert and Martina's. For the life of me, I could not see how she could not see my point. I could not understand why this is the stance she took. I prayed on it and asked God for guidance. This is a person I love so much. Who is more than just a friend. Do I just let it go? Over twenty years of friendship. Do we talk about it? What is there to talk about? We've been down this road before. She's choosing them. She's always choosing them. Toward the end of the three months, I was at the point of contacting her to request a sit down. She beat me to it, and sent a text inviting me to lunch. I accepted and we met at our usual spot. She sits across from me, once again catching me up on the recent events of her life. I'm mainly quiet cause most of the stories involve partying and reconnecting with her long lost sister, and some new found friends. Well she sure as heck don't need me I remember thinking. She was inviting me out with her new friends and I wasn't about that life anymore. I was out of the club scene. It was the same thing from five years ago. I had my fun, now I was more than content to stay home curled up in bed reading or watching tv with some wine. After she talked, I explained to her that I did a lot of thinking since the last time we spoke and I am once and for all removing myself from the equation. I realize how important Martina and Robert are to her, and I am giving them custody of her and will just bow out.

Our friendship is one I cherished. It meant a lot to me, and she still holds a special place in my heart. We shared a great portion of our lives, and have a million shared memories. It's been six years since that lunch. I've reached out to her a few times. Mainly because I do miss her, but she doesn't answer. At first I used to call hoping to wish the kids a happy birthday, but that never happened. I'd send birthday wishes to her kids through mutual friends but that's it. As always I wish her well, but I think that is it for us. I still hope to be in touch with her someday, but being as stubborn as she is, I doubt that will ever happen.

# MY SURVIVAL

*"My mission in life is not merely to survive, but
to thrive; and to do so with some passion, some
compassion, some humor, and some style"*
— *Dr. Maya Angelou*

P EOPLE OFTEN ASK how I got through it all. My answer has always been as simple as four little words. It wasn't a choice. I never woke up in the morning asking myself, are you getting out of bed today? Do you think you can do it? That was never an option. I simply woke up, thanked the Lord for His grace, and got our day started. I placed one foot in front of the other and kept them moving. I am not audacious enough to think I made it alone. I made it with the help of the good Lord, and the guardian angels he placed in my life. The one who knows my destination before it's even revealed to me. I made it with the help of the village that helps me raise this tribe of mine. There was no way I would have made it from there to here without backup. That is something I had in abundance. Be it Jasmine who has been my lifesaver from jump. I can't ever remember a time I asked her to watch the kids for me that she said no. This is a woman who I owe so much to. Having her in my life permitted me to go to clinicals every week. I was able to study because of her. When I started working she's the one who was consistently able to watch the kids when I needed without fail. She was even more amazing once I started traveling for work. I would be away for weeks on a contract and could count on the kids being safe with her.

I had my sisters of the *Women With Books*. The book club started the year before the separation. We met once a month for discussions. We were a group of professional women who were friends and enjoyed the pleasures of reading. At the end of each meeting, there was a segment called "Sisters, Help Me." It was during these segments one of us could talk about anything we needed to talk about. I can tell you that I practically monopolized these "Sisters, Help Me" sessions, these women were phenomenal. If I needed to be heard, they sat there and listened. If I needed advice, there was no shortage of that either. They were there for me and helped keep the demons at bay.

My sister Yolanda has been a rock for me. She's been there through it all. I can remember the days at her house, my efficiency days and nursing school days when it was hard to make ends meet. She was always there. There were times I would cry thinking, I'm the older sister, I should be the one helping you. Not the other way around. She'd remind me this is just a patch I'm going through and things will be fine before I knew it, and she was right.

My mom through all of this has been a mama bear. She doesn't care that I am forty-three years old, she still tries to protect me from the world. If I get obnoxious and get annoyed at her over-protectiveness I laugh at myself thinking I do the same with the kids. As a mother myself, I know if I'm fortunate enough to be one hundred years old I'll be exactly the same way. So I cut her some slack and let her do her mothering thing. It's a knee-jerk reaction for her. There's no age limit to stop worrying about your children. Thinking back on the early days of the divorce, leading to the betrayal, she had taken it so hard. She lost so much weight, wasn't eating and cried often. Regardless of how much I'd tell her I was fine and the kids and I were ok. She felt it too, the hurt and the pain. She's a great human being. She is kind and über generous. Everyone who knows her love her. She's a great mom and an even better grandma. I love her beyond measure and thank God for her every day.

I can't begin to name everyone who's played a part and have been there for me over these last few years. I have a wonderful group of friends and family. In spite of it all, I refuse to stop trusting people. I do believe that people are innately good. We just lose our way sometimes and all it takes is for another soul to notice and provide the necessary guidance. I truly have been blessed. It's not luck, it is blessings. Plain and simple. His blessing rain down on me on a daily basis and I am forever grateful. The human in me is not worthy, but that doesn't seem to stop Him one bit because he knows my soul. The amount of gratitude I have is as infinite as His love is.

# MY SUN MOON, AND STARS

*"A mother's love for her child is like nothing else in the world. It knows no law, no pity, it dares all things and crushes down remorselessly all that stands in its path."*
— *Agatha Christie, "The Last Séance"*

COMING FROM A family as big as mine, I always had a lot of cousins around. Because of this, I always knew I wanted a lot of kids. Six to be exact. Yes. 1, 2, 3, 4, 5, 6. That's how many kids I wanted. Don't know where that number came from but that's the number I always had in my head. Meeting Robert, he was down with it. At least he was at the beginning. So we ended up with four instead, and that was fine. Four is perfect actually. I tell people all the time, I have two pairs, and that is a winning hand in Vegas.

These loves of mine are truly heaven sent. The good Lord knew I would need purpose to go on my life's journey so he blessed me with these four beautiful souls. That's what they are. My purpose. I cannot tell you how lucky I feel to have them call me mommy. That is one of my favorite words. Mommy. They are the reasons I wake up in the morning. The reasons I pushed forward when I have no strength to do so. All I would need to do was think of one of them and my spine would straighten if it started to slouch. It's amazing how they renew my spirit on a daily basis. Every little accomplishment has been for and about them. Nursing school was for them, the struggles to be better has always for them.

More than anything, they're good kids. Even though I can associate every grey hair on my head to one of their shenanigans, I wouldn't trade them for anything. That is to say, they're not perfect, but they're perfectly mine. I remember Robert trying to fight me for this and for that during the divorce and all I kept thinking was you can have it all, just leave me the kids. Just leave me, my babies. He wanted the bookshelves in the office, the Tiffany lamp downstairs, the paintings he had picked out. He wanted to take so much. He felt entitled to take it all, but all I wanted were my babies. Other than some clothes and a few pictures, I didn't care about any of it. Things can be replaced. If a hurricane hits tomorrow and took it all away, I'd be thankful to come out of it with our lives and that's all I kept thinking. We're alive and well. Take whatever you want. Just give me my babies. Today, most of those things he fought me tooth and nail for, are in his mother's garage collecting dust, or laying around her house. What good are they now?

He loves the kids, I can't deny that, but it makes me wonder. Where was the love when we were living in the efficiency apartments? Where was the love when we were getting evicted out of our apartment? My brother in law

Sam spent hours well into the morning helping me move on numerous occasions. Not once did Robert ever volunteer to say you know what Roxie, I can come and help you move. We always manage though because God never left us. My God is good all day every day. Through it all, the kids never went hungry. After 2008, I never received a red cent from Rober Gaultier in child support, yet they ate and had a roof over their heads. People constantly ask me why I don't go after him for child support. Why? I would ask. You can't get blood from a rock is my usual response. God has always provided for us, and He will continue to do so. The Robert I married isn't the Robert the kids have grown up with post-divorce. I'm not sure who this Robert is. I want so much for them. During the separation/divorce, my heart ached for them. I wanted to take the pain away from them. To take theirs and make it mine. I needed to find a bubble to put them in to keep them from going through it. God always knows them better than me. He's always had them under His wings.

# THE BACK STORY

*"Those who cannot remember the past*
*are condemned to repeat it."*
*— George Santayana*

IT'S JANUARY 1994 I am living in Estero, FL with my mom and sister. It all started in a little night club in Punta Gorda, FL. Before *The Spot*, there was The *Rooftop*. It was our Saturday hangout place for reggae nights. This particular Saturday was New Year's Night. I had been visiting my cousin Val in Sanibel, and we just had to get to *The Rooftop*. It's all we could talk about. The thing is, her sister Vicky was getting married the next day, but we were set on making it work. We're all hype on making it a great night. Me, Val, her boyfriend Dale, and a couple more of her close friends. After a long line, we get in and it was great as usual. We weren't old enough to drink yet so it was all clean sober dancing and fun that night. While dancing, I noticed a guy crouching in the middle of the dance floor. Who does that? I wondered, then I dismiss him as weird, and keep dancing next to my cousin and her boyfriend. A few minutes later, someone is dancing behind me. I look over my shoulder, and it's crouching tiger from earlier. He was keeping up, so I shrug and kept dancing. After a while I yell over my shoulder "How old are you?" as people tend to do at the club to be heard over the music. He lifts his left arm revealing his twenty one and over armband. "So? I respond "anyone can get one of those." "Twenty one" he replies, and we keep dancing. "How old are you?" he asks back. "Fifteen" I lied smiling. With that he puts his hands up and pretends like he's about to back away. I grab him by his shirt collar to bring him back and say "I'm kidding, I'm nineteen" I laugh. We spent the rest of the night dancing. He cracked a few jokes which made me laugh, and before we knew it, the lights were coming on, cause it was time to go. Don't know where the time went. He walks me outside and we talk a minute. We introduced ourselves, and he asks for my number. I never liked giving guys my phone number. So I told him to give me his, and I'll call him. Something I had no intentions of doing. "I have sisters he says, I know how the I'll call you deal goes." "No, I will call" I say now only half lying. If he's calling me out, I'll show him. He was skeptical but wrote his number on a piece of paper. "You don't even have any place to put it he pointed out eyeing my outfit" I was wearing a tight fitting black and white bodysuit with a black short shorts with no pockets. I take the piece of paper and tucked it in my bra. "I have a secret pocket" I say smiling. He laughs, and we parted ways.

It is after 6 am as we head back to Sanibel. Vicky was getting married in a few hours. Val and I are supposed to be ushers in the wedding, but we still didn't have our dresses because the dressmaker never finished them. We make it back to the Sanibel area by 7 am and the search for our dresses started. The only problem is, everywhere was closed. It's the first Sunday of the year, and of course, nothing was open. We head back to her house empty handed leaving us to wear our own backup black dresses. The kicker though is black was not part of the wedding colors. We're back at her house getting ready. I take off my bra to shower and something fell to the floor. I pick it up, and the small piece of paper says Robert and has a phone number scribbled on it. It's that guy from *The Rooftop*, I smiled. I was about to crumple it when I remembered how sure he was that I wouldn't call. "Let me call him real quick just to show him," I thought. I dialed his number and he answers. "Hello, can I speak to Robert please?" "Who's calling?" he asks "This is Roxie" I answer. "Roxie who?" he asks "Oh, you got jokes," I say recognizing his voice. He laughs and says he's surprised I called. "I told you I would" I said. We only talk 10-15 minutes, because I have to finish getting ready. It only took that much time for me to know I wanted to talk to him again. That's all it took.

I called him the night I got back to Estero and we talked for hours. We didn't have cells at the time so landlines and pagers were it. That's just how we communicated back then. I didn't have a boyfriend at the time but I was dating this guy Owen, and he was someone I was thinking about getting serious with. Meeting Robert changed all that. At first, I figured I'd keep seeing them both to see where it would go. One day, I made plans for the both of them to pick me up from work without realizing it. It wasn't until I was walking out of mall where I worked I remembered. I hid and asked the security guard to let know when either of them get there. If they both got there at the same time I was screwed. Robert came first and I went with him. He knows the story. Years later he would ask me what would have happened if Owen showed up first. We would joke I would have been Mrs. Owen instead. The truth is, I would have chosen Robert regardless. I fell hard for him, so I broke it off with the Owen and never regretted it. That was it. We were madly in love. He was a great guy, super funny and romantic. He wrote me poems and gave me love songs, it was great. I always felt like the most beautiful woman in any room with him.

Our love continued to blossom. Back in 1994, it was long distance to call outside of your town and we lived in different cities. He was in Bonita Spring, and I was in Estero. He became very creative. He would drive to the local hospitals and call me from the waiting room, and I would buy phone cards. We couldn't get enough of each other so three months later, I proposed to him while we were taking on the phone. He said yes but we should finish school first. We continued taking classes and booking hotel rooms to see each other. In October 1994, We found out I was pregnant. We hadn't been trying but it happened. We were both happy but also knew the major ass whooping waiting for us by both parents. If you know anything about Haitian families, you know the predicament we were in. The 'don't get pregnant in my house rule' was universal, but for the Haitian family, that was the law. We were both working so we decided, no big deal, we're grown. What can they do to us? We'll just get married sooner, get an apartment, have our baby and live happily ever after. Being the responsible (ha!) young adults that we were him 22, me now barely 20, we rented an apartment, and set our plans in motion. Now all we had to do was tell our parents. I told my mom first. She didn't take it well. My mom is a very emotional person, so it was all tears, and you're trying to kill me, what will people say. We still had to wait a few days before our apartment was ready so I moved in with my friend Isy while we waited cause home wasn't the place to be at the moment. Now Robert had to tell his parents. They wanted to have a sit down. I'm thinking "Mézanmi" (my goodness gracious). This wasn't their first time meeting me. By then we'd been together 9 months and I'd been to their house multiple times, and I was close to his little sister Cassie who was the barely 10 at the time.

The question now is what do you wear to go speak to your boyfriend's Haitian parents to discuss the fact that you've been having unprotected sex with their son and are now pregnant as a result? It had to be something they couldn't interpret as slutty. So, I decided to go with a light blue skirt and matching jacket except with my tiny baby bump, my size 7 skirt would not zip up. I went with that outfit anyway hiding the open zipper with the jacket. The truth is most everything else was at my mom's and I wasn't about to get killed. We made it to his parents', and that meeting didn't go so well either. I think they were holding back a little, saving the real to give to Robert when they're alone with him. They weren't as emotional as my mom, but they laid into us regardless. You guys are so young. Why the rush? You need to focus on school and on they went. So, for now, we are on our own. We moved in late on Halloween night after we both got off work with the help of his friend Eddy.

Two weeks later, on November 17th I miscarried. Neither of us could believe it. We had been so excited, and just like that, the baby was gone. I was 11 weeks along. We'd heard the heartbeat just weeks before. Our hearts were broken. I don't think we told many people right away. Two weeks after the miscarriage on November 29th, we walked out of the local courthouse a married couple. We were over the moon. Our families couldn't understand why we got married even though we lost the baby. Only my grandma understood. It was never just about the baby we tried telling them. The baby just sped up the process. The plan was to have a big wedding on our 5 year anniversary, but that didn't happen. We got too busy having more kids and decided it'd be best to use any money saved for a house.

The early years of our marriage were great. We were getting used to married life and enjoying each other. I don't think I could boil water when we got married. Robert taught me how to cook. My mom did all the cooking and cleaning at the house growing up. We worked a customer service job together. He left after a few months, I stayed 9 years until the company went out of business in 2003. We became pregnant again in the summer of 1995, and 9 months later we were blessed with our first child, little miss Priya Roxie. She was born on valentine's day. A gift to the both of us. All of our valentines day until we were divorced were always gladly shared with her. By the time Priya was 9 months, I stopped going to school and worked more. Robert, however, continued with school and work. We wanted to save for a house so we moved in with his parents six months after Priya was born. Robert lost his job and was out of work for almost a year so that set us back some on the savings front. Once he started working again, we moved into a couple different apartments while we continued to save for a house. This more or less is where my fluctuation in weight started. If you know me, you know I'm not highly concerned about my weight, though I should be. Back then I somewhat was. I still carried an additional 25 or so pounds from the first 2 pregnancies. My family had no problems commenting on it. Perfect strangers would comment on it. "Oh Roxie, what happened? How did you gain all this weight?" It's called having a baby asshole I wanted to say to them, but being a nice Haitian girl, I'd smile, shrug and walk away. Mind you, I was 5'7" weighing 160 pounds. I'd kill to weigh 160 pounds today, but whatever. Robert would make comments but never to make me feel bad. Well, at least not then.

In November 1999 the beautiful little miss Indya Roxie was born, baby number 2. After having her, my weight went to a whopping 200 pounds. Whoa!!! My family will never let me live that off so I was on a quest to lose the weight quick. With the combination of diet exercise and diet pills prescribed by a doctor, I was down to a size 4 in no time. An all-time low for me. That didn't last long though. I stabilized at about 150 pounds and I'll be damned if I still didn't get slack for it. After all my efforts and weight loss, we became pregnant again with baby number 3 just a few months after Indya turned one. We also managed to save enough to build our first home. We closed on our townhouse in June of 2001, and four months later welcomed our first son Quincy Robert in October 2001. At this point, I was well over 200 pound after giving birth to Quincy, and I was determined to achieve the weight loss success I had after Indya. That was without success, though I made it to about 180 pounds, I was done trying. I was done having people talking shit about my weight and wasn't killing myself anymore. Not the best argument but it's the one I got.

From then on my weight was always an issue. It has been the one aspect of my life I can't seem to get a good handle on. The one aspect I'm not able to muster up enough willpower to overcome. I know I have it in me, I just can't seem to channel it right. Once in a while, if a group at work would start some fad diet, I would participate. I'd do it for a while, and stop after getting frustrated from not seeing any results.

Robert worked more and more and was often home very late. We stopped spending time together. He helped with the kids and around the house, but time together just us was almost nonexistent. I was no Suzy homemaker. I am not now nor have I ever been a great housekeeper. Anyone who knows me knows that about me. What I don't do myself, I will hire a professional to do, or I will get to it when I get to it. I have no qualms about it. He would like to paint a Peggy Bundy picture of me, as if I was this kept woman. I wish I knew that was an option.

I remember 'Roxie day'. This came about because of the lack of quality time. He was always running off somewhere, so I asked for a Roxie day'. We talked about it and he agreed. It was supposed to be one day a week that was only about me. If anyone needed his help for something it'd have to be done before or after Roxie day. Well, that never happened. After the first day, he decided he was too busy to give me an entire day. We tried counseling, but were kicked out, well he was kicked out. He thought he knew more than the counselor who was a woman. "She doesn't know what she's talking about" he would say when she would point out a flaw to him. She asked me to come alone next time and told me she can't help him but would gladly continue individual sessions with me. I asked him if we could find another counselor he declined, so that was it.

In 2003, the company where I worked for almost 9 years was going out of business and I was laid off. Talk about a shock to the system. I collected unemployment for a short time while looking for work. I was also going to school and graduated from the local community college with an AA in Mass Communications. The plan was to transfer to the local university for a BS in the same field to pursue a career in public relations. Robert was making a good living, but I needed to find work. We eventually sold the townhouse, and moved to an apartment while waiting for our next home to be built. At around the same time, Martina and Max moved in another building of the same complex. That made it easier to see each other and hang out. Things would get better with us only to slide back to being stagnant. All these times we remained very social, getting together with our friends on a weekly basis. This Friday at our house, next Friday at Martina and Max', then Jim and Elizabeth's and so on. We were all so close. The guys had their investment group, and us ladies would have spa days and lunches. We were hosting our annual NYE parties wherever we lived. We were healthy, our kids were healthy. We had great friends and family, and everyone loved us. Life was good.

After losing my job as a customer service manager, it was difficult finding work. I was either overqualified or not qualified enough. So, I became a realtor. I did odd jobs for a couple different temp agencies on and off. I was a receptionist, personal assistant and so on. The costs associated with real estate was too much, so we agreed to let the licence go. After real estate, I started a party planning business "Events By Roxie". This was something I was good at. I was planning parties for family and friends already, so why not focus on that. We'd compare the cost of child care for three kids with the salary I could potentially be making going back to work full time and decided that I would get the party planning business going and keep the kids home. Business was doing well. I was building my clientele, and creating rapports with vendors. I was getting good contracts, and then I became pregnant in the middle planning 2 big weddings.

The weddings were about 2 months apart, and in June 2006, Sebastian Robert made his debut on our family room floor the night the Miami Heat won their first NBA Championship. That was only a few weeks before the second wedding I was planning. Ever tried telling a bride you need to take it easy at the wedding they hired you to plan because you just gave birth? Yeah me neither. I took the baby with me, muscled through it, breastfed when during cocktail hour or whenever I could, and went home 10 hours later with swollen ankles and leaky sore nipples. It was a week or so later Robert came home and gave me the news that he was leaving.

ROXIE GAULTIER

# LOVE AFTER HEARTBREAK

*"Nothing in the universe can stop you
from letting go and starting over."*
— *Guy Finley*

I DIDN'T HAVE A whole lot of dating experience before I was married. There was my high school sweetheart Trevor. We were together for two years and it was intense. The entire school knew of us. Always kissing and making out in the hallway. Even the teachers grew tired of us. He had our entire future mapped out, only thing is I didn't know what I wanted to do. He was my first long term boyfriend. Yes I loved him, but how did he know I was it? I wasn't sure he was it. I was sure I loved him, but I wasn't ready to play house. I wanted to go find out who I was. So towards the end of senior year I told him we should break up after graduation and see what happens. We did just that but he was very reluctant. I went to canada for the summer and came back knowing for sure I wasn't ready to settle down. I was only 17 years old for crying out loud. Soon after, he dated and married a close mutual friend.

Almost 2 years later, I lost my virginity to a friend. He was someone I didn't associate love with, and that made him perfect. We both worked at the mall. One day I looked at him and thought, why not him? We used to ride to and from work together. Just like that my mind was made up. I was almost 19 he was 26. Most people I know wanted their first time to be someone they love, for it to be special blah blah blah. What if they break-up with you later? I used to think. You're always going to associate that with this person who broke your heart. Not me. I never wanted that. Maybe that was part of the reason I never went 'all the way' with Trevor. So after getting the deed done, I met Owen and nothing happened with him, then Robert came around and that was it. That was the extent of my experience pre-marriage. I didn't truly get introduced to the dating scene until after my divorce.

Since my divorce I've dated, been in relationships and have fallen in & out of love. I for sure knew I didn't want to get married ever again. I mean the first one was supposed to be forever. I used to joke that the first time was for love, and the second time would have to be for money. I mean, how could I trust anything else to last now? The divorce was too hard. I couldn't imagine putting myself through that again. Not to mention there was the factor of the kids. How could I bring a man in the house as my husband? What if they don't vibe? I'd pick the kids. It would always be the kids. Would that be fair to this new person? I didn't care if it would or not. The only way to deal with it is to not marry anyone. Problem solved.

I'm not sure how healthy that thinking was but it worked for me, and the good thing is that never became a problem.

Now though, I think of it often. Probably because the kids are getting older and are one by one starting their lives and don't need me like they used. It would be nice to have a partner, a companion to finish it all with. I am finally open to that possibility. That's another favorite word of mine. Possibility. If we open ourselves up to it, the possibilities truly are endless. I am ready to enter a new chapter of my life and begin again.

# EPILOGUE

*"Thank you for coming on this journey with me"*
— *Roxie Gaultier*

AS I WRITE this story, I am 43 years old living in Port Charlotte, FL with my children and two dogs. The girls are 22 and 18. Priya is now an incredible yoga instructor who is on her own journey of self discovery. She is indeed a beautiful soul. My indigo child. Indya is in her first year of college. She's not far from home so we can just hop in the car for a quick visit. She is sweet and loving but acts like she's Mr. tough guy. She is bright and wise beyond her years. She's quite the mother hen when it comes to her siblings. The boys are 16 and 11. Quincy is in his sophomore year of high school and has his own personality. He stays to himself a lot but when I least expect it, I'll get a hug and kiss here and there. Sebastian, the baby of the family is an old soul. That is the best way to describe this little boy. He's driven and has lots of plans. He's very creative. He thinks he is either my father and or husband. Leave it to Sebastian to say what everyone else is thinking. Fearless is what he is. He and Indya are the most territorial when it comes to me. If I didn't say it before,

I'll say it again. These little kids are my sun moon and stars. I can't imagine this life without them.

As for me, I am still here. I am surrounded by a loving and supportive group of friends and family. I thank God for putting them in our lives. They are always there for the kids and I, and always have our backs. I work a lot in order to give them everything they need. I am ever so grateful to God for seeing me through it all. It is only by His grace I am able to bring this book to fruition and be able to share my experiences with you. My hopes for this book is for it to reach anyone who will find something from experiences. Be it hope, strength, or even a little humor. If it reaches anyone and can make a difference in their lives then I will be a happy woman. I am still learning at every single turn. My journey is only beginning. I keep God at the center of our lives and He has never steered me wrong.

Thank you for reading.

CPSIA information can be obtained
at www.ICGtesting.com
Printed in the USA
LVHW041135060219
606577LV00001B/177/P